Interperson<!---->

Importance of relating <!---->

By Alex Canny

COPYRIGHT

The information presented in this report solely and fully represents the views of the author as of the date of publication. Any omission, or potential Misrepresentation of, any peoples or companies, is entirely unintentional. As a result of changing information, conditions or contexts, this author reserves the right to alter content at their sole discretion. The book is for informational purposes only and while every attempt has been made to verify the information contained herein, the author, assumes no responsibility for errors, inaccuracies, and omissions. Each person has unique needs and this book can't take these individual differences into account.

This book is copyright © 2019 by the Author Alex Canny with all rights reserved. It is illegal to copy, distribute, or create derivative works from this ebook in whole or in part. No part of this report may be reproduced or transmitted in any form whatsoever, electronic, or mechanical, including photocopying, recording, or by any information storage or retrieval system without expressed written, dated and signed permission from the author.

Table of Contents

Introduction .... - 1 -
Chapter 1: What is it? .... - 3 -
Chapter 2: Why do you need it? .... - 12 -
Chapter 3: Side-effects .... - 22 -
Chapter 4: Are you ready? .... - 26 -
Chapter 5: Learn / Cultivate .... - 34 -
Chapter 6: Application .... - 51 -
Chapter 7: Networking .... - 55 -
Chapter 8: Interpersonal Intelligence in Practice .... - 58 -
Chapter 9: Career Options .... - 68 -
Chapter 10: Larger picture .... - 71 -
Conclusion .... - 74 -

Introduction

Have you ever heard someone say "He is good with people" or met a person who has a ton of friends and I'm not just talking about Facebook friends, I'm saying friends they meet with, or go places with, on regular basis.
I'm here to tell you this is not an accident, anyone who has a thriving circle of friends or dedicated colleagues was either born with a particular type of character or developed the necessary skills to end up in such a position.

The lucky ones are people you've interacted with since you first set your foot outside your parent's house. I'm talking about the child who walked up to you on your first day of school and invited you to sit next to them or introduced you to their circle of friends.

Later on in life, these naturally inherent character traits serve them to increase influence, get further up the professional ladder and achieve goals faster. These individuals usually go on to become leaders in politics, religion or business.

The good news is that you don't have to be born "with it" in order to enjoy the benefits of having a high quotient in interpersonal intelligence.

Anyone can learn how to develop the same traits and skills to, not only take advantage from associated benefits, but also to grow as a person, increase emotional strength, and become a happier and more fulfilled individual.

This book will take you through a deeper understanding of what Interpersonal Intelligence is and why you should aim to build or increase it as well as step by step instructions on how to do it.

Chapter 1: What is it?

Definition

The subject of Interpersonal intelligence has been studied and written about in one form or another throughout the ages. Some of the oldest references date back to great philosophers such as Aristotle.
In more recent history books such as "How to Win Friends and Influence People" by Dale Carnegie first published in 1936 opened our eyes to how important people skills are in society. This book was so successful it sold over 15 million copies, which puts it on the bestseller of all time list, and remains in high demand even today.
Eventually coined by Howard Gardner in 1983, Interpersonal Intelligence and other intelligence types have changed how we perceive and quantify the term 'smart'.

This topic transcends cultures, language, and nationalities, its basic principles are present in every part of our life, whether it's in the office, factory, at home or playground. The dictionary defines Interpersonal Intelligence as the "ability to communicate or interact well with other people", but it's so much more - it's also the ability to read and influence others, to have empathy, and to know when to speak and when to listen.

Nobody is as a stranger to a person with high emotional intelligence; they will start a conversation with a person sitting next to them on the train and make them feel like they've known each other for years.

How to identify it?

Although hard to quantify, Interpersonal Intelligence shines brightly in people who possess it and if you know what to look for, you won't miss it.
Everyone has these individuals in their lives, you might even be one of them, but to make things easier I've put together two lists for you.

Before you read the lists, understand that we all have varying degrees of interpersonal intelligence and nothing is exactly black and white, the lists merely demonstrate extremes on both ends of the spectrum.

Traits of a person with HIGH Emotional Intelligence;

- great listener,
- collaborator,
- inspires others,
- sensitive to the needs and moods of others,
- adapts to different situations,
- great communicator,
- gets away with saying 'no',
- has lots of friends,
- enjoys meeting new people,
- master in the art of persuasion,
- people often confide in them,
- enjoys social interactions,
- has few enemies,
- team player,
- initiates conversation,
- people follow them,
- often invited to events.

Traits of a person with LOW Emotional Intelligence;

- socially awkward,
- avoids social interactions,
- confrontational,
- avoids meeting new people,
- shows low empathy towards strangers,
- adds *'fuel to fire'* in a heated situation,
- doesn't like change,
- scared of being 'wrong',
- prefers not to participate in meetings,
- small circle of friends,
- you really have to get to know them to like them,
- treats new colleagues like enemies,
- introvert,
- rarely plays teams sports.

Statistics and studies

The last two decades show a significant amount of research involving multiple intelligence, and how it affects our progress through life. Early studies centered around education and learning styles; they showed how our natural (stronger) intelligence type can impact how we receive and understand information.

Based on a survey carried out by LinkedIn in 2018, with over 2,000 business leaders in 100 cities showed that soft skills were at the top of potential candidates' skill gap.

The data identified the following three as most critical:

- Leadership,
- Communication,
- Collaboration.
-

All 3 skills are an integral part of interpersonal intelligence.

In 2017 Google wanted to see which teams were the most effective and productive. They carried out an internal study which revealed - to their surprise - that the best performing teams were not the ones with best engineers or most skilled analysts; Google's top teams were made up of individuals with strong soft skills. It's these soft skills that were attributed to having the biggest impact on success, especially during the collaboration process which forms the basis of every project.

An MIT Sloan study shows that soft skills training in the workplace - regardless of whether carried out in a blue or white collar environment - greatly improved productivity. Some of the factories taking part in the study reported up to 250% ROI within less than a year.

How to measure it?

The number one indicator and easiest way to measure interpersonal intelligence in a person is by the number of friends they have, and secondly by the lack of (or few) enemies.
A person with high interpersonal intelligence has an ability to make you feel at ease and open up, even if you naturally put up walls to keep people out.

These are obvious signs of interpersonal intelligence, but in reality, it's a hard thing to measure, which is why it's often overlooked and not valued whilst we're still at school. It's so much easier for the educational system to identify 'smart' individuals - based solely on their ability to reason, remember, and be good with numbers.
But what is defined as 'smart' in school no longer serves you as you start your first job or get ready to climb the ranks in your career.
Individuals with high IQ believe - which was enforced by many years in education - that they are superior, unfortunately, this attitude stunts their personal growth and closes doors to professional advancement.

It's at this point that 'smart' people start to rebel; they don't want to come to terms with reality - and the reality is that they need to learn new skills in order to expand their social network, meet new people and be able to collaborate effectively.
They don't understand why the promotion they've been working for so hard and deserved, was instead given to the funny guy (a.k.a. The office idiot).
People with high Intellectual Quotient (IQ) and low Interpersonal Quotient often become depressed as they enter

the workforce, which often leads to substance abuse and other addictions.

There are a lot of cases of people gifted with both (or more) types of intelligence, the 'unicorns' of this world, these individuals have the potential to move mountains.

Quick Examples

In the book "The Tipping Point" by Malcolm Gladwell, he describes three types of personas; the maven, connector, and salesperson.
All these personas have varying degrees of interpersonal intelligence, but I would rank the Connector as highest, Gladwell describes this person as a "people collector" and a trendsetter - this individual likes people, knows a lot of people, and as soon as they see someone who could benefit from meeting one of their contacts, the Connector introduces these individuals to each other.

In life we see many examples of people with high interpersonal intelligence, we see them in our leaders, organizers, hosts, game changers, and what is commonly now referred to as 'Influencers'.
People like Nelson Mandela, Barack Obama, Mother Teresa, Oprah, and more recently Gary Vaynerchuk among many others all share common threads of being able to gather a vast number of people around them, who become their loyal fans.

These individuals are involved in all sectors and at all levels, you'll find them wherever there's a group of 2 or more people connected by either a profession, goal, hobby or initiative.

Chapter 2: Why do you need it?

The benefits of developing interpersonal intelligence are too many to count, they can help us to achieve great things for ourselves and for those around us.
This is particularly true in relation to big projects. Large ideas require the skills and talents of many in order to turn them into reality.
The number one talent of people of influence is the ability to gather and harness the skills and talents of others with the aim of fulfilling great (and small) dreams.

Some of the benefits relate to small seemingly insignificant things and occur on a daily basis, the way we relate to people we interact with, in shops or pass on the street.
Without uttering a word, so much is said when a young person gives up their seat to an elderly person on the bus -

they have no idea how much this little 'gesture' impacts the way they are perceived by all other passengers on that bus.

Some of the most ancient civilizations have coined words such as Karma to describe the benefits (or consequences) of how we interact with and treat others. Christianity often refers to loving your neighbor the way God has loved us. Today, most children would have heard their parents tell them to treat others the way they'd like to be treated. Some parents go a step further and ask their children to put themselves in the shoes of the child they're having a dispute with, to see the situation from the other child's perspective - now that's great parenting.

This chapter is divided into 2 sections: Professional & Personal, as both of these overlap into every other area of our life.

Professional

Our chances of a fulfilling and successful career depend on our ability to bring more to our job than just our expertise. It's more evident than ever that soft skills play a critical role in our capacity to land a better position, with a higher salary and better benefits, not to mention more flexible working arrangements.

Landing the Job

This process starts as early as the recruiter gets our resume, it's obvious that our hard skills will take center stage of the CV, but our references are what really brings it home.
It's the people we have worked with/for in the past and their opinion of us that is ultimately going to decide whether we win the race for that job against other equally skilled potential candidates.
The more 'leverage' we can generate with our collection of great references, the more negotiating power we'll have during the interview and final employment contract forming process.

First Job

Young people often blame lack of experience to explain their inability to find a job in their chosen field, even while holding university degrees. Many give up and end up working at McDonald's or some other job that's 'beneath' them, others take some time off to 'find themselves'.
What these individuals don't understand is that they might already have enough in their arsenal to get them over the line for their first job.
They undervalue the 'projects' they worked on with their classmates, or the article they wrote for the school paper, or the after hours (slave) labor they performed at their parent's shop or babysitting their neighbor's children.

Next Jobs

Once people get a few years in the workforce under their belt, the number one mistake they make is that they approach employers from a position of weakness, only thinking about what's NOT on their resume.
They completely underestimate the power of charisma and their personality, which shine through during any interactions they have with a potential employer or recruiter.

Whether you're applying for your first or fifth job, you need to emphasize your social skills and use them to sell yourself at the interview. Most employers are now aware of how important soft skills are in the workforce and many value your personality and your potential to thrive in the existing company culture over your professional experience or qualifications.

Career - Progress

Your ability to thrive and excel in your position will depend on how fast you can learn, expand and apply interpersonal intelligence.
The best strategy is to develop a long-term plan for your career, then reverse-engineer it to identify the people and skills that you'll need to get you there.

You'll need to figure out who's reference you'd like to add to your resume, then be of service to that individual. Some of you may find this manipulative or outright call it "ass-kissing", but my job isn't to tell you what you want to hear, it's to tell you how reality works and what you need to do in order to get where you want to be.
The real talent of a person with high interpersonal intelligence is to be able to keep their views and opinion to themselves in order to not alienate others, who may have different beliefs.

Whilst you are making friends with the people who can help you get to the next level, don't ignore the 'little people' you work with, they can turn into powerful allies and have your back in case you ever need it. Remember that they are also likely to be consulted by your superiors as references for your next promotion.

Business

Interpersonal intelligence will equip you with the perfect skills to get clients, but not only for a quick sale, but long-term raving fans of your venture.

If you play your cards right, they will become a client of any future businesses also, because people don't stay loyal to brands, they stay loyal to the values these brands represent and the people behind them.

As an example, Apple has following many other businesses are envious of, this is due to Steve Job's relentless strive for quality and top design, he never compromised his drive for perfection, even when his own job was on the line.

In business, you'll be constantly dealing with people, in all types of situations and at all levels. You'll need all of the following skills and then some, to not just survive, but to succeed;

- Sales,
- Negotiation,
- Hiring,
- Firing,
- Listening,
- Making decisions,
- Dealing with pressure,
- Market mentality and expectations,
- Target customer and their character,
- Be aware of others emotions/states of mind,
- Carry out performance reviews,
- Provide constructive criticism,
- Provide encouragement,
- Identify individuals with potential and enable them to grow,
- Guide and mentor others,
- Provide clear instructions,
- Develop lasting relationships with all types of personalities.

There will be times where you may need assistance from outside your workplace or industry. Having powerful friends in other circles is not just a strategy but a must for your professional success.

You can achieve this through networking events or any other time you meet with people outside of your usual environment. Take advantage of every situation to add these names to your contact list, then schedule in time to develop and maintain these relationships.

These relationships may not always benefit you directly, but indirectly by making something important happen for your boss or client.

Tom Peters, a world-renowned business management consultant, author, and speaker is often quoted saying that the power of your influence is directly proportional to the thickness of your Rolodex.

He says that you should never eat lunch alone, best use it to meet someone new, or get to know a colleague better who works in a different department in your company, or better yet at a competitor's company.

Personal

The ability to work and collaborate effectively with others is especially helpful in a workplace environment, but that doesn't mean you can't enjoy the fruit of these skills in your private life.a
Interpersonal skills can serve you when you interact with your friends, your spouse or other family members to e.g. organize a trip, plan Christmas or move house.

Our character, mood, and personality affect how we act, but most importantly it affects others - in a positive or negative capacity respectively.
When we cultivate and actively work on ourselves it helps us become better people and makes those around us are happier, which in turn positively affects us even more - it's a snowball effect.

Long-term Relationships

The ability to develop lasting relationships is often an undervalued skill, but it's where you can reap the most benefits directly connected to happiness.
Everyone's idea of success is different, but for the most part, we are drawn towards activities which bring us pleasure and move away from anything associated with pain.
Close and intimate relationships are where we draw our greatest joy and pleasure from, so it makes sense to invest in them and do everything you can to strengthen and help them grow.

Intimate Relationships

Some people are a great fit for each other, which makes sense when they decide to enter into a long-term, intimate relationship.

The problem is that, when you don't have the skills required to read people and understand what motivates them and drives their decisions, you're likely to enter into this type of relationship with the wrong person.

You may start to date a person, who pretends to be someone else, or worse, pretend they like you just the way you are. Knowing how to read your potential mate and knowing the signs to look for before you get too emotionally involved can save you from a lifetime of heartache or discontent.

The same skills can help you identify someone you could be really happy with (and them with you) for many years to come.

Chapter 3: Side-effects

Newton's law states that "for every action, there's an equal and opposite reaction" and it's true, who we are and how we act, affects not only us but everyone else we meet or deal with on a daily basis.

How Have You Changed

Have you ever heard a spouse say: "that's not the person I married" - whether we like it or not we all change, and if we don't actively work on how we'd like to change, we default to changing for worse.
This is a natural occurrence, whenever something is neglected it deteriorates, that's the way life works.

It's in our nature to choose the path of least resistance, to choose what's pleasurable, not difficult, hence so many people fall into addictions (pleasure-driven habits) even when we know that the consequence of that path leads to pain for us and others.
Our primal brain isn't able to process the meaning of 'future', it only understands NOW and demands immediate gratification - and it becomes very good at improving the speed of getting from 0 to 10 on the pleasure scale.

Luckily we all have will power, but more importantly, we have an image of ourselves - an image of who we believe we are, and where we see ourselves in the future.

Our Hidden Power

The only thing more powerful than the desire for pleasure and immediate gratification is our story. The story about who we truly are, our values and beliefs.
Our subconscious mind is like a slave, it will do everything it can to conform to that image, it will make you act and say things to align yourself with that picture.

For example, if you've ever desired a particular car, let's say it was a Mustang, your mind immediately knows it's something that's important to you and it will make you take notice of it whenever it's in your environment - others will not even know it was there, but you noticed.
We can use this to change and acquire new habits, but more on that later in chapter 5.

Our Choice

Whether we see it or not, we are faced with a fork in the road on a daily basis, some of us have trained ourselves to make a decision so fast they don't even see the fork anymore. There's actually many forks, and each one represents a decision, will I press the snooze button, will I smile to my partner, how will I respond to their request for assistance, will I let a car in my lane, will I say hi to the jerk-off in the next door cubicle?

The list is long, and each time we make these millions of decisions they cause an effect and take us in a different direction, even if it's not evident right away.
You can use your influence to either help and empower or destroy, encourage or criticize - the choice is up to you.

Chapter 4: Are you ready?

The same way you can't paint a room without first preparing its surfaces, it is also with us when we decide to change our behavior and take on new habits, we first have to take a moment to prepare.

Studies show that around 50% of what we do on a daily basis is done on autopilot, we have developed strong neuro-connections, which have default settings on how we act and respond to situations and people.

That's why it's crucial to step back, take a deep breath and reflect on what needs to be done before we can proceed to the next step.

Prime Yourself For Learning

Some people are more pliable than others, they have a natural ability to evolve - others struggle with the smallest change.
Regardless of which group you belong to, there will always be a transitional period of preparation or priming, which will increase your chances of taking on new habits.

Step 1

We're going to start this process by looking inward.
The first step is to identify your own social behavior habits, everything that you do on autopilot when interacting with others.
The intention is not to judge, but merely to take note of your learned behaviors.

Become your own observer in every interaction with another person and pay attention to the following:

- How you act,
- Where you stand (proximity to the other person - in relation to personal space),
- Your conversational style (e.g. do you ask questions or talk about yourself)
- Your facial expressions,
- Your posture,
- Do you maintain eye contact?
- The tone of your voice,
- The pitch and volume of your voice,
- Percentage of how much you speak vs. how much you listen,
- How much do you repeat yourself?
- Do you cut in and don't let the other party finish their sentence?
- Do you finish their sentences?
- Do you say what's on your mind?
- Are you diplomatic or do you say it how it is,

This list is just the beginning of what happens during a standard conversation, please write down answers to these points as well as other behaviors, which may show up during the interaction/s.

Step 2

This time, we're going to look outward.
I'd like you to do the same exercise, but this time direct all of your attention on the person/people you're interacting with.

I'd like you to notice how they are reacting to you - take a look at:

- Their facial expression,
- Their tone of voice,
- Are they maintaining eye contact?
- Are they leaning towards you or leaning backward,
- Do they roll their eyes?
- Are they nodding their head?
- Are they loud?
- Are their eyes sparkling? or glazed over,
- What is their posture?
- etc.

I'm sure by now you understand where I'm going with this. You don't have to limit yourself to the above list, I encourage you to add as much detail to your observations as possible.

Step 3

Now that you have done step 1 & 2, sit down and evaluate your behaviors. Draw two columns, in one, write down which behaviors (in your opinion) serve you and in the other column, each one you'd like to change.
Identify the state of mind you were in during those interactions; were you well rested, happy, grumpy, tired, hungry, etc...

Next, prepare another list, this time write down the other party responses from your social interactions; in one column list all behaviors you were pleased with, and the ones you found less desirable, in the second column.

Look at the ones you liked, try to identify what you did to evoke such a response.
Now take a look at the less desirable ones, reflect on your words or actions, to what degree did they contribute to the manifestation of these negative responses.
Did you provoke them? Or were their responses guided by a mindset they already had prior to your interaction?

Now I'd like you to prepare a third list, this time next to all the responses from the other party, list all corresponding emotions you think that person had during the course of the interaction.
For example: eyes glazed over = bored, facial expression = smile = happy/pleased/good mood.
Write them down even if you're not sure what they were feeling at the time.

Step 4

You first need to understand the reasons behind the way you act as well as what you say and how you say it. What's driving these behaviors?
Do you have a default setting for social interactions, are you usually: upset, happy, depressed, angry, sad, silly, defensive, have low energy and are always tired, are you a complainer and talk to others about all the horrible things that have happened to you.

You need to realize that it's not just the state of mind you were in at the time of these conversations, but biases you had about the person.
Another important aspect of your behavior is driven by your beliefs about who you are - not just in general, but also in terms of you vs. them, i.e. are you their boss? colleague? sibling? parent? etc.
All these factors will affect the style and dynamic of these interactions.

Prepare another list, this time write down your physical and emotional states, biases, perceptions, and all the other factors I mentioned above.

Now challenge some of these, are your biases all correct? What if you changed some of the dynamics, how would that change their behavior and outcome of the conversation.

Step 5

As you prepare yourself to go to the next stage, realize that a lot of your social behaviors have been adopted by you either intentionally or by default from your parents when you were too young to remember or make an informed choice.
They are not necessarily all good, and if you want, you can choose to change them, just remember that no matter what kind of adjustments you'd like to make in your behavior, don't lose the part of you that makes you, you - we are all a little weird and that's what makes us unique amazing individuals - always stay true to your own style.

Ask yourself why you want a change, but also why you wouldn't want to change, you have to acknowledge the subconscious mind, and it's hardwired to protect you from anything new, including new behaviors. Be prepared that as with all changes, your subconscious will try to revert you back to your old ways, and will try to sabotage your efforts.

You have to accept that the new behaviors will feel alien and unnatural at first, it's only when you recognize these feelings of resistance for what they are, that you'll be able to succeed with your character building changes.

You have to associate strong feelings with this new decision and utilize the power of imagination to see yourself in different social situations and acting it out on how you speak, listen, and respond to those around you.
Like a well-trained athlete you repeat this over and over until it starts to feel natural, then and only then you promote yourself from simulation into a live test run.

When you're ready and want to give your new skills a try, I suggest you first go to a place that less threatening, somewhere safe where you won't feel embarrassed.
For some it's in front of the people closest to them, for others, it's a place full of strangers they will likely never see again.

Chapter 5: Learn / Cultivate

Before you can learn or apply these new habits into your life you first have to learn how to control your own emotions. You'll need to increase your level of Emotional Intelligence in order to apply Interpersonal Intelligence. Because it's only when you're fully aware of your own mindset and triggers that you are able to enter emotionally charged, negative situations, and turn them into a win-win for both parties. Emotional Intelligence isn't the subject of this book, but I highly recommend reading up on it as it can really help you excel in developing your social skills.

The Rule of Reflection

According to Anneli Blundell, an expert on interpersonal intelligence also known as people whisperer, people are wired to respond to your level of expectation. What she means is that if you think someone is a bit of a loser, they will act like one when interacting with you - on the other hand when you have respect for the other person, they will act according to that belief when around you.
She claims that just by changing your perception of the other person, you will change the biochemistry of the interaction, which will cause both of you to act differently.

Your Social Circle

I'd like to start with the most important and most useful advice on how to cultivate Interpersonal Intelligence in your life.
If you weren't born yesterday, you have heard the saying: "birds of feather flock together", which refers to the fact that you become who you spend time with.
One of the strongest animal instincts we are born with is to mimic the people closest to us, the ones we interact with the most. This is how we naturally learn as it's the easiest way to do it; a shortcut.
To use this shortcut put yourself in situations which allow you to spend time with individuals of high interpersonal intelligence, then observe, mimic and learn. Soon you'll find yourself acting like they do and reaping the benefits.
The only warning I have is that everybody has flaws, so make sure you don't pick up the bad with the good, be actively conscious of which actions you want to mimic and which ones you'd like to avoid.

Mentor

We all have mentors in our lives whether we're aware of it or not, although we may not call them that.
A mentor is just a big word for someone we respect and want to learn from. It doesn't mean we want to be 'just like them' but we'd like to adopt some elements of their character which appeal to us.
Some of us use this correctly and apply what we've learned from these individuals, whether through a personal relationship or from afar (from books or listening to their talks).

Karma

Treat people well and with kindness, because the way to treat them teaches them how you'd like to be treated.
Research supports this claim, people reflect back on to you how you treat them - good and bad.
This works in intimate relationships as much as around the office, remember this next time you want to make a mean remark, even if that person actually deserves it.

Active Response

Our brain isn't designed to make good decisions under duress, I'm not saying that we're not capable of doing it, I'm saying that making a decision in a stressful situation should be avoided whenever possible.
Our creative/problem-solving part of the brain performs best without all the cortisol floating through our system and for some people who have not had any training in this area, it shuts off all together under duress.
This is when we as humans make the worst decisions, the hulk comes out and he does not listen to reason and doesn't care about consequences, let alone the feelings of the those around him.

Don't make rushed decisions in the heat of the moment, sleep on it if you can. But if due to time restrictions you can't, at least take a quick time out by stepping out of the room for a moment or going for a quick coffee.

The same can be applied to a conversation, in this case, your emotional state may not be so intense, but sometimes a single word can cause a lot of damage and what has been said cannot be unsaid even if we try to apologize or try to convince the other person that we didn't really mean it.

Don't respond immediately in an emotionally charged conversation, bite your tongue if you must. Take a moment or two to answer.
Some of the following responses will acknowledge their feelings and may diffuse a conflict;

- really? I had no idea....
- I didn't realize I came across this way, it was not my intention,
- I think I screwed up and didn't express myself correctly,

Don't be defensive, agree with them - this is their truth.

If you find it hard to get a handle on your emotions during a confrontation, use your body (breathing, movement, posture) to change your state - this changes your biochemistry and will help you to think a little clearer.

Let Go

Let go of your hurt, when people hurt others, it's always due to the issues they have, it's not about you.
Whenever you hold onto hurt, you give away your power to the person who caused the pain. You are the master of your own life and the mistakes of others, their problems and character faults are not.
See the situation for what it is, if you have contributed to the problem in any way, own it and figure out how to apologize and learn from the situation, so that you don't repeat the same mistake in the future.
What you can't do is blame yourself for what the other person did, this is on them, they are entirely responsible for their words and actions.

When you feel hurt, learn to control the pain by redefining the situation, and by actively working through the pain. If you leave a wound unattended it will get infected and cause more damage than the initial injury.
Time does not heal all wounds, it just makes us a little numb to it and if you don't deal with emotional pain in your life, it will strike at the most inconvenient moment or sabotage your future happiness.

Dealing with Bullies

Most people will at some point in their life (not necessarily at school) have to deal with a bully.

Bullying is a form of sadism, meaning that the perpetrator takes pleasure in the pain of their victim. They use various means to cause pain, but the most common is through words. The most effective way to disarm a bully is to agree with them - this is one of the exceptions in life where you don't speak the truth.

When confronted by a bully, keep calm and repeat what they say in some form or another or try diffusing it through humor e.g.
- you're ugly,
    - Yeah, I know I'm not front page material,
- you're dressed like it was Halloween,
    - It's not? Damn it!
- I hope you die,
    - You know I did have a stomach bug the other day, maybe my day has come,

Hostility and hurtful words aimed at humiliating you is the only thing a bully has, and when you agree with them you take away their ammunition - and when the gun is filled with blanks, it cannot cause any damage.
This the quickest and most efficient way to make them give up. They don't get what they want, which is seeing you suffer and they lose interest.

You can also use this tactic to diffuse a conflict or heated situation.

No Thanks

Getting out of difficult questions and situations are some of the most valued skills in the political arena. This behavior is defined as being 'diplomatic'.

As mentioned earlier, one of the character traits of people with high interpersonal intelligence is that they get away with saying "NO".
They have the ability to decline all types of requests with tact and in a way which respects the other person.

Bob Burg, a bestselling author, has one of the best formulas to say NO, which I use on regular basis, it goes: "Thank you so much for asking, while it's not something I'd like to do, please know that I'm honored to have been asked"
If the person persists, you can say: "I'd rather not, but thank you so much for asking"

Off course you can use your own variation of these words, but it's a perfect way to allow the other person to save face and not make them feel rejected, but to also allow you to get out of doing something you don't want.

Just because you're a nice person, doesn't make you a doormat and you have the right to decline any request for your time or assistance.

Deals

Often portrayed in movies, the art of negotiation is one of the most admired traits, not just on a professional level, but also in personal life.
The ability to read the person sitting across from you, to understand what drives them, their limits, and what's it going to take to come to an agreement, are some of the skills required at the negotiating table.
It makes no difference what kind of negotiation it is, whether you're negotiating a high profile corporate merger or buying a car, you'll have to engage your interpersonal intelligence to come out successfully on the other end.
According to the world's most respected professional negotiators, 'successful' doesn't mean I win - they lose; the aim is almost always for a win-win outcome on both sides.
Top negotiators spend years sharpening and expanding their skills, experimenting with what does and doesn't work.
Chris Voss, a former FBI negotiator, says that it can take as little as one specific word (spoken by the other party) to induce a biochemical reaction in the person you're interacting with and open them up and listen to what you have to say.

The phrase he is referring to is *"that's right"* instead of *"you're right"*. According to Voss, when the person says *"you're right"*, they are really saying *"please stop talking"*, they're being polite but don't want to change their position, they just want you to shut up.
You have to figure out a way to get them to say *"that's right"*, what this means is that they feel understood by you, a chemical reaction takes place in their brain which suddenly makes them receptive to your point of view and open up to what you have to say, and they don't even know why.

Chit Chat

Improve your verbal communication, in particular, the words and phrases you use as well as how you express them - your tone of voice, volume, posture, facial expression, general body language.
Practice in front of a mirror or record yourself to see how you come across. If you (or someone that has your best interest) think that adjustments are required, then go ahead and make those adjustments, then practice, practice, practice.

Remember that you don't always have to share your point of view, find common ground instead. We all like to talk about ourselves when meeting someone new, but it's better to be the one asking questions with a new acquaintance.
Use your questions to find what unites you rather than what pulls you apart, then use that to build further rapport.

Look for verbal clues (sometimes it's just one word) when engaging in conversation. Words such as "I'm unsure about" sometimes mean "I don't want to" or "what are we going to do with" means I don't want to put myself in a vulnerable position.

The quickest way to give someone a confidence boost is to ask them their opinion. It lets the other person know that they are important to you and you value them as a person. It also implies that you think they are smart, which elevates their self-esteem and strokes their ego, and stroking someone's ego isn't necessarily a bad thing.

My last tip is one of the most important; Use people's names when addressing them. Research shows that we love nothing more than the sound of our name spoken by another person. Use this and other tools to elevate the person you're engaging with to make them feel important.

Visual Cues

A study by Mehrabian & Wiener, 1967 and Mehrabian & Ferris, 1967 divides communication into verbal on non-verbal cues with a much higher percentage given to the latter. The exact numbers (since widely adopted) were 55% for body language, 38% for the tone of voice, and 7% for the actual words.
This has now been disputed by many, saying that this formula cannot be applied in all situations, which has been confirmed by Mehrabian himself.

Nevertheless, it clearly proves that we assess the people we interact with on more than just words. We make split-second judgments about the people we meet based on the way they dress, walk, their tone of voice, and million other clues our brain has picked up on without us even knowing. It does this in order to form a story about who this person is, what they want, and whether we're going to like them.
Our brain is doing this to help us decide what we are going to do, it's formulating a story about the other person; is interacting with this person going to be safe, fun or something else.
All of this focuses on ourselves, it's looking inward, in order to develop our Interpersonal Intelligence, we need to start looking outward, at THEM.

As much as these assumptions are generated on auto-pilot we need to stop and intentionally analyze the person in front of us.
How do they stand? Straight and tall or slumped over - observe their shoulders, the energy with which they move. What about their breathing? and the speed with which they speak....

Pay attention, these are all little clues about how they feel, and what they are 'really' saying.

Don't stop there, observe their reactions and how they respond to what you're saying, are they interested? Bored? Annoyed? Happy?

In order to improve on your communication skills, you need to learn how to actively observe others when they communicate with you, but also to pay attention to how they respond when it's your turn to speak.

You never know what you can pick-up on - maybe nobody has ever had the guts to tell you that you talk too much, or that your breath stinks etc. People will keep a lot to themselves out of being polite and not wanting to hurt your feelings.

If you don't know what you're doing right or wrong, you will not be able to break your pattern and become a better communicator and people reader.

How Can I help You?

There are few things more powerful than meeting someone's needs or solving their problem, or just being there when they need you the most.
We value these grand gestures, but mistakenly undervalue the little things we do, which show that we pay attention, care and value the other person.

A leader's primary job is to help others do theirs better and a good leader measures success by how many people they help. They recognize talents and natural gifts in others and help them to cultivate and incorporate them into their work.
This, in turn, makes their job a lot more fulfilling, which positively affects their performances and loyalty.

Many studies confirm the "law of reciprocity", which states that when anybody does something nice for us, we have a hardwired urge to respond in kind, often in a greater capacity than the original act.
Please be careful and not abuse this law, people know when they're being bought, only do this out of genuine motive - never use this to get something in return. This law only works when you give without expectation.

Expectations

What you'll also notice in individuals with high interpersonal intelligence is that whenever they interact with another person they don't have expectations about how they want the other person to act and respond.
They understand that this only sets you up for disappointment and may cause conflict. Although we are human after all and will automatically be driven to have expectations - when this happens, try not to hold that person to those expectations, but adapt to the situation and don't allow yourself to be let down.

Always Look Your Best

Remember that just because you're learning interpersonal intelligence doesn't mean others will. And first impressions will always be the most important thing others will use to create a story about who you are and decide whether they will want to interact with you or at what level.
I even tested this theory out in the emergency room where I stayed for hours (on more than several occasions) observing who received better (and faster) treatment.

Consistently the people who came in with scruffy hair and in their pajamas or 'home clothes' ended up with far worse treatment by the triage staff than the ones who took 5 seconds to look at least half-decent. I know this isn't fair, because you don't exactly think about dressing nicely when it's an emergency and you are really unwell, but these were my observations. Don't take my word for it though, here is a link to a Forbes article confirming my findings.

Know Thyself

The first thing that comes to mind is the plaque hanging over the door in the Oracle's kitchen in The Matrix (1999 science fiction movie).
Self-awareness is 'step one', it's your key to unlocking all other parts of your life, it's understanding your worldview and values.
You need to have a good sense of self-awareness to answer the basic question of what makes you happy.
Which activities make you feel fulfilled through and through, where do you naturally thrive.
What makes you laugh and what makes you feel ashamed or embarrassed.

All these questions and more start at the core of knowing who you are and what drives you.

In order to interact with others, you'll need to identify your own emotional triggers. You don't want to be caught off guard when somebody accidentally (or not) presses your buttons. You need to anticipate these situations, see yourself responding - not reacting.

The more you learn about who you are, the more you'll be able to make informed decisions about where you're going and which path you'll choose to get there.
But most importantly, you'll be able to identify who you'd like to take along for the journey.

Chapter 6: Application

The applications of Interpersonal Intelligence are endless, but I'm going to list the most prominent ones and divide them into 2 main areas of your life; personal and professional.

Professional Life

At work

- Use your new skills to contribute or help build a better company culture,
- Deepen current relationships with other people at your company,
- Extend circle of outside allies,
- Deepen relationships with clients,
- Help the company gain new clients (even if it's not your job),
- Learn from the best,
- Mentor a new employee,
- Get involved in side projects,
- Volunteer for tasks outside of your job description, but offering a chance to expand your skill-set,
- Do small favors for your colleagues,
- Improve a process at work,
- Take full advantage of work events to expand your network of friends,
- Invite a colleague from a different department to lunch,
- Develop a training course,
- If the company doesn't have one, produce a new employee onboarding document/email,
- Wash the coffee cups in the sink,
- Treat work trips, training, and conferences as an opportunity to meet more people,
- Contribute to a safe work environment,
- Be an example.

In Your Business

Most of the above also applies to your business, below is a list of additional items;
- Develop HR policies and courses,
- Give your employees the right tools to do the best job they can,
- Pay attention to the atmosphere at work on a daily basis,
- Ask others for their opinion (especially people working under you),
- Acknowledge the accomplishments of others,
- Elevate others (give credit where credit is due),
- Attend outside networking opportunities,
- Develop relationships with powerful people,
- Keep on learning,
- Learn how to hire/fire people correctly.

Personal Life

Our identity is intertwined with how we perceive ourselves within the context of family and close friends.
You're a son, a daughter, a brother, sister, father, mother, a friend etc...

We can use our newly acquired skills for the following:

- Support others in pursuing their dreams,
- Enable them to reach higher,
- Constructive feedback,
- Help them overcome challenges,
- Guide them how to break their destructive patterns,
- Counsel them when needed,
- Help them adjust their path,
- Be there when they need you,
- Help them develop constructive coping mechanisms (e.g. go for a walk instead of open a bucket of ice cream),
- Put others before yourself,
- Pay attention to their feelings and needs,
- Bring a 'happy you' to every situation,
- Do the little things (dishes, take out the trash),

Chapter 7: Networking

Some people collect stamps, influential individuals do the same but with people, except for them it's not a hobby, it's a life strategy. It's not by accident that the most powerful and successful people in the world have a contact list running into thousands.
Tom Peters; best-selling author, international speaker, and a world-renowned business consultant says that your Rolodex is the most valuable asset a person can poses.

Networking seems such a big technical word, but all it really means is interacting with other people (new and existing contacts) to develop further relationships.
The skill of networking entails the ability to walk up to a complete stranger and strike up a conversation or better yet, have a mutual friend introduce us to them.

Whenever you find yourself at a traditional networking event, use it as a training ground for you, utilize this environment practice, learn, and observe, you can never learn too much when it comes to the science of social interactions.

The idea is to never miss an opportunity and practice this skill any chance you get. Most of us associate networking with a special event or a conference, but opportunities to network are around every corner.

Making new acquaintances can open new doors and provide access to people you would've otherwise never had a chance to meet.
Networking doesn't necessarily require you to be at any particular place or event, all you have to do is to pick up the phone and ask your friend, who knows a friend to give them your number.

Here are some places you can use for networking purposes:

- Sitting next to someone on a bus, train, plane (make sure you do it with respect and give them an out if you see that they just want to be left alone),
- At your kids birthday party (when the parents drop or pick their kids up),
- Conferences & Seminars,
- Common interest-based meetups (meetup.com),
- Whilst standing in a long line,
- Church,
- Waiting rooms,
- And many more....

Always be ready and well presented, because you never know who's going to cross your path. It makes no difference if you're just going down the street to buy milk, there are no excuses for not looking your best.

Chapter 8: Interpersonal Intelligence in Practice

This chapter is dedicated to real-life examples of interpersonal intelligence in action.
The following examples of people in everyday situations in different roles: as colleagues, employees, bosses, siblings etc.

All of the examples are true - but people and company names have been changed to protect their identity.

The Real Estate Broker

Sarah has just received great news, she's going to be the new real-estate broker at a large national realty chain.
This particular branch was only a small office with 8 staff members. Nevertheless, she really wanted to make her mark and succeed and not waste this opportunity.
She knew that even with 9 (10 including herself) people there will be a good mix of personalities, which means a high probability of possible future conflict.

She knew that in order to have the success she wanted she was going to need the support of the people working there, so she decided right there and then that in spite of not having even met all of them yet, she was going to like all the team members regardless of who they will ultimately turn out to be. No matter what they will do, say, even if they show hostility towards her, talk behind her back - nothing was going to change the decision that she likes them.

As soon as she started working there, she looked for the good in all the people she worked with; 2 bosses, 1 manager, 2 receptionists, the bookkeeper, and 3 other salespeople already working there.
All these people had flaws, they had plenty of days when they were grumpy, unpleasant, and at times, jerks. But in those situations, Sarah took her ego out of it and did not take any of it personally. She always tried to understand what motivated these actions and didn't react emotionally.
It was one of the best decisions she has ever made, within 12 months she became one of the top-selling brokers in the nation, won her first awards, and made lifelong friends in the process.

The Hiding Manager

Jeff just hired a new recruit Adam, who showed a lot of potential. A few weeks later Jeff started to avoid him, he said: "I can't have a conversation with him he just goes on and on about how great he is, I can't stand when people boast, this is driving me crazy!".
This couldn't continue as Jeff was Adam's direct manager and interacting with him was a part of his job, so he consulted an expert who proposed Jeff take the following two steps to remedy this situation.

The first step was to just start having little conversations, try to keep them short and sweet, Jeff said he could do that, but it was the second step that posed a huge challenge, the expert asked Jeff to start praising Adam: "You want what?!" Jeff exclaimed.
The expert went on to explain that there must be a reason for this kind of behavior, and the most likely answer is that Adam must have some confidence issues, for which he overcompensates by talking about how great he is.

Jeff followed the expert's advice and tried step two, he started to compliment and praise the new recruit for any job well done.
A few weeks went pass and Jeff noticed a significant reduction in Adam's bragging behavior, in fact, everything about his boastful manner started to calm down.

The Screaming Match

A new production manager was hired for a manufacturing factory that was having a lot of problems meeting delivery schedules. Up to this point, everything was done by the factory manager Louis, and the only people who worked at

the factory offices were support staff such as designers and admin.
Louis was the one running the show and only reported to the operations manager who came down from headquarters once a week to check on things.
So when the new production manager Fred, was hired to help put the factory back on schedule, Louis saw him as a threat and as someone who wanted to challenge his authority at the factory.

Fred started the job knowing that he will be the new 'man in charge' and after meeting all factory staff he realized what he is up against.
Having prior experience with this type of challenge, he decided to adopt a "servant leadership" style, in which the main role of the leader is to serve.

He started with factory toilets, the stark difference between the office and factory toilets were undeniable and it wasn't right - so he rolled up his sleeves on his first weekend there and whilst every factory worker was enjoying their time off at home, he fixed the broken mirror in the toilets, then cleaned everything from the floor, through to the toilet bowls. He even went out and bought the screws missing on the toilet seats and screwed them back on.

He was the first one in every morning and the last to leave at night, within two weeks the factory was starting to get on top of the schedule, materials were being ordered on time and everyone knew what they were supposed to be doing on any particular day.

Fred got along really well with all staff and was well liked, all except one person, he knew that Louis hated his guts. So he devised an unconventional plan to reassure Louis's sense of authority and allow him to show everyone that he's still boss (at least on the factory floor).

One day an opportunity presented itself, Fred needed something done urgently and Louise was unavailable, so Fred went over his head, straight to the delivery, by which he was changing the schedule him and Louise already established for that particular day.
You see, it's not that Fred didn't have the authority to do this, but Louis was very touchy about Fred going straight to the guys as he wanted to be the one to give orders around the floor.

But Fred knew what he was doing and this was an intentional act to stir up Louis, to push him over the line, and push he did. When Louis found out what happened he became furious.
One of the factory guys came into Fred's office and told him. Right away Fred came down to the factory floor, he wanted to catch Louis in the heat of the moment, it worked.

Louis started screaming at the top of his voice, saying a lot of words starting with the letter "F", Fred just stood there nodding his head, then in a calm, but loud enough tone that everyone could hear he said "I'm so sorry Louis, I shouldn't have done this without consulting you first". After which, he turned to go back to his office - "You go back to your little office! And leave the factory to me!" Louis screamed.

Fred was pleased, everything went as planned, Louise didn't talk to him for the rest of the day, but when they met the following morning to plan the day ahead, Louis was a different man - cooperative and friendly. Fred allowed him to get his dignity back and show the entire factory that he still has authority.

A couple of months later when everything was on track again, the HQ called a meeting to see if they still need to keep the production manager.
Louis was one of the people invited to the meeting, they discussed a few things, but when the subject came up of whether the production manager should stay on Louis jumped to his feet and said "No Way! you cannot fire this man, you have no idea how much things have improved at the factory and how hard he works to make this place run like clockwork, we need him! if you let him go, you might as well fire me also".

Fred was in shock he knew that things have been really good between them since the 'screaming' incident, but he had no idea how much bond has developed between them. Long story short, Fred kept his job, until he moved onto the next thing, but he and Louis are friends to this day.

Snobby Colleague

You can't make everyone like you, but you can try.
When Anna started at her new admin job there were four other admin girls already working there. They usually ate lunch together, three of the girls welcomed Anna with open arms and invited her to lunch with them, meanwhile, Jess ignored her completely.
Anna tried very hard to befriend her, she was nice to her and always said hello. She did all the normal things that you do to try and befriend someone at work.

After about a week when that didn't work and Jess was still ignoring her - she was obviously treating her as an intruder. So Anna tried a different tactic, she started to ignore her as well. At lunch she wouldn't even as much as look at her, she just talked to the other women as if everything was normal. This worked like a charm, it only took 3 days for Jess to warm up to her. She started saying hello to Anna in the morning and chatting to her at lunch.

Just because most people will respond to a friendly manner, doesn't mean all will. Some people respond with a smile when greeted with a smile, others get suspicious. Your job is to figure out which one of these people you're dealing with and find a way to get through to them regardless. The key is not to take their attitude personally, which would ruin any chance for a future relationship.

A person with high interpersonal intelligence sees beyond convention, they know that the norm doesn't always work, you have to see the person in a different way to figure out what drives them.

Construction manager

Tim worked for a joinery company, which had a contract to provide all cabinetry for a large construction project of a 4 story building apartment in a major city.
Tim was the project manager on this contract, but the factory was running behind (and so was the construction project) in manufacturing all the required joinery.
The project was coming to an end and everyone was feeling the pressure from the developers to get it finished fast.

David, the Construction PM was the one responsible for the entire project and if he didn't finish that weekend, his company was going to face huge late penalties.
He hired extra installers to work over the weekend to finish installing the last pieces of joinery, he really needed them to be delivered before the weekend.

But the factory (including its owner) was not in a rush, they kept on pushing the deadline every day that final week, they did manage to finish all the pieces on Friday afternoon, but as the clock turned 3 pm, they refused to deliver what was needed to site.
Tim called David and told him what the situation was, but said that even though it's not his job, he will deliver all the pieces himself.
He paid two younger workers to stay a bit later and help him load the truck, they went home, but Tim went to the building site; he arrived at 8:30 pm, David and the installers team were waiting.

Because of Tim, David was able to save face, avoid penalties, and finish the project that weekend.

Fast forward around 12 months, Tim was ready to move on. A position became vacant at the very construction company that David worked for.

David was widely respected by his peers and his opinion mattered, when it came to references he was consulted about Tim.

Tim got the job, when he asked, what was it that put him over the line, he found out that David spoke so highly of him that they had no other choice than to hire him.

Grateful sister

Frank and Sarah were just normal teenage siblings, one night Mum asked Sarah to do the dishes after dinner, Sarah had something planned and really didn't want to do it.

Rather than say NO to her Mum, she approached her brother Frank.

Sarah: "Can you do the dishes for me tonight please"
Frank: "nope"

They were standing a little farther apart and she couldn't hear him very well, she was 100% sure he said: "yep"

She turned to him with the most gracious, happy smile of relief she said: "Oh, thank you so much! You're an awesome brother"

At that point, he froze for a moment, he really didn't want to do the dishes, but at the same time - she was so grateful, he didn't want to disappoint her, and as much as siblings like to tease each other, at that moment his sense of decency kicked in and he ended up washing the dishes.

I'm not sure whether it's true she heard him say "yep", but it shows how much a person's expectation can make you do things you didn't want to do to begin with.

We are all different with varying biases and stories about life. A wise person makes it their job to figure these out. It doesn't matter whether it's work or Christmas with your family, you'll need the assistance of those around you, so it just makes sense to have as many allies as possible.

Chapter 9: Career Options

A quick online search for the most in-demand skills will reveal Soft Skills rise to the top of the list. In a CNBC interview in May'18 Jeff Weiner, LinkedIn CEO said "somewhat surprisingly, some people may not realize [that] interpersonal skills is where we're seeing the biggest imbalance"

Soft skills are in high demand in all sectors, we are at a point where they are valued more in white-collar positions, but blue-collar recruiters are increasingly on the hunt for these also.

Seth Godin, best selling author, and authority on marketing and social sciences goes as far as to say that the word 'soft' is inappropriate.
He argues that "culture defeats strategy" and what really brings success to companies is the number of employees with strong soft skills, which (to their demise) most employers still view as optional.

Right Person for the Wrong Role

A good leader is great at reading people, and when they see that a person is not well suited for a particular role, they are able to have an empathetic but honest conversation about other options.
Stay open to constructive criticism of others, sometimes it's the people we work with on a daily basis who are able to see our talents or shortcomings better than us. Remember that as long as you follow your own calling it's never too late to change careers.

Best Career Paths

Here is a list of the most common career paths for people with well developed interpersonal intelligence:

- Counselor,
- Social Worker,
- Teacher,
- Athlete - Team Sports,
- Trainer,
- Salesperson,
- Psychologist,
- Poker Player,
- Host - Events,
- Wedding Planner,
- HR - various positions,
- Manager (at every level & in every sector),
- Politician,
- Concierge

Plus many more, the best roles for individuals with strong soft skills are in positions involving reading, dealing with, and influencing people. So don't limit yourself to the above list, the opportunities are endless.

Chapter 10: Larger picture

Once you learn interpersonal intelligence it starts to become second nature, you can't unlearn it. And the more you use your new skills, the better you get at it. It will also make it easier for you to learn other types of intelligence.

Become a master at reading other people, take some lessons from professional poker players, they spend years learning and perfecting this art. To become really good at this, you'll need to learn how to identify cues even when people are trying to hide what they're feeling.

Once interpersonal intelligence becomes a part of your new identity, you'll mature and understand not to judge a book by its cover. Our primal nature tries to protect us from threat and predators and it forces us to make an instant assessment of someone's intent and character the moment we see them. As you grow your skills you'll understand that there are many layers to a person and you won't be at the mercy of those primal impulses, which will allow you to give everyone a second chance at a first impression.

Just like cars need maintenance, we also need a checkup once in a while - sit down regularly (e.g. once a year) to evaluate where you are to make sure you're on track with your external and internal goals.
Reflect on your current situation and recent events, check yourself; have you accidentally picked-up any new bad habits? What new improvements you'd like to make? what new traits you'd like to adopt?

Our brains are elastic, we're only limited by the stories we tell ourselves about who we are and what we're capable of - you are the only one who can remove the limit and be free to become the best version of yourself.
The more we learn and keep our brain active the easier it is to learn other things such as a new language. Studies have also shown that learning new skills slows cognitive aging.

Having high interpersonal intelligence can save you from years of heartache by being able to recognize the right person to enter into a long-term relationship with.
The benefit of being able to read others allows you to recognize your potential partner's true feelings to see if there's a future for this relationship.
What's driving them? What expectations do they have from a future spouse? Do they love you just the way you are or are they hoping you will change? Will they want children? How often do they want to have sex? How do they feel about money management within the context of a couple?

Having the right skills will also make these potentially explosive conversations run smoother and without long term negative effects. Having a high level of interpersonal intelligence allows you to make hard decisions, which in the end benefit all parties involved.

You will not notice it right away, but if you keep at it soon your entire world will change. People will start to respond to you differently, your opportunities will increase and success will become your constant companion.

Conclusion

As a school child, you are told to sit down, shut up, and don't talk to anyone - especially your neighbor. Don't get me wrong, I'm grateful for the education I received, I only wish we were allowed more interaction and I don't mean during breaks, I mean to learn in pairs, in groups.

The only way we can thrive as a family, community, or a business is through relationships. The ability to flourish in social interactions and have the skills to create friends, not enemies is one of the most powerful intelligence of all.

I encourage you to grow, to live with intent and purpose, have a plan for your life, be kind to those around you and be self-aware and present in every moment.
We must let go of negative connotations associated with

persuasion, we need the skills to influence someone to make good choices - having this new power is like coming to a lot of money, money is not evil in itself, you just have to ensure you use it for good.

Learn how to sustain and expand your new skills through journaling and daily rituals.

Leave the past in the past, the person you were yesterday is not the person you are today. Smart people find ways to learn, reflect, and improve on an ongoing basis, it's how they live their life.

Never lose your youthful curiosity and enthusiasm - wire your brain for success and position yourself for happiness.

Thank you for reading this book.

-Alex Canny

Made in the USA
San Bernardino, CA
09 June 2020